A Cowboy's Faith

Text and paintings by

Harvest House Publishers

Eugene, Oregon

A Cowboy's Faith

Text Copyright © 2001 by Jack Terry

Published by Harvest House Publishers

Eugene, OR 97402

Library of Congress Cataloging-in-Publication Data

Terry, Jack, 1952-
    A cowboy's faith / Jack Terry.
         p. cm.
    ISBN 0-7369-0679-7
    1. Cowboys--Religious life. I. Title.

BV4596.C65 .T465 2001
242--dc21

2001016949

Artwork designs are reproduced under license from © Arts Uniq'®, Inc., Cookeville, TN and may not be reproduced without permission. For information regarding art prints featured in this book, please contact:

Arts Uniq'
P.O. Box 3085
Cookeville, TN 38502
800-223-5020
www.artsuniq.com

Jack Terry Fine Art, Ltd.
25251 Freedom Trail
Kerrville, TX 78028
(830) 367- 4242
www.jackterryart.com

Design and Production by Koechel Peterson & Associates, Minneapolis, Minnesota

Scriptures are taken from the Holy Bible: New International Version®. NIV®. Copyright © 1973, 1978, 1984 by the International Bible Society. Used by permission of Zondervan Publishing House.

Printed in Hong Kong

01 02 03 04 05 06 07 08 09 10 / NG / 10 9 8 7 6 5 4 3 2 1

Dedication

To our daughters and their husbands, Kelly and Mike, Paige and Shannon—
To our grandchildren, Hunter, Haley, Jordan and Drew—
"Let your light shine!"

Special Thanks

To my dad, Frank Herring—
For being such a tremendous role model, truly a man after God's own heart

Contents

jackTerry ©

Together, We Can Make a Difference

Now faith is being sure of what we hope for and certain of what we do not see. This is what the ancients were commended for.

Hebrews 11:1,2

My grandson Jordan recently celebrated his fourth birthday. For many days preceding the joyful event, he anticipated with great excitement all of the presents he would receive from his friends and family. As we gathered around the picnic table in the backyard with cake, ice cream, and balloons, Jordan was certain of what was going to happen. Although he did not visibly see the gifts before the party, he was confident that he was soon going to open lots of presents, just like he did at last year's celebration. His faith was strong because his previous experience had been a very real one. He was sure of what he hoped for and certain of what he did not see. This is a wonderful picture of the simple, childlike faith that God desires for all of us to have.

God made this hope available to every person more than two thousand years ago when He tore down walls that had divided nations from the beginning of time. Jesus proclaimed, "A new command I give you: Love one another. As I have loved you, so you must love one another. By this all men will know that you are my disciples, if you love one another" (John 13:34,35). He went on to say, "I have given them the glory that you gave me, that they may be one as we are one: I in them and you in me. May they be brought to complete unity to let the world know that you sent me and have loved them even as you have loved me" (John 17:22,23). This is the common ground shared by those who desire to please God.

Faith, hope, and love are the threads that bind believers together in unity. While Christian unity does not allow for division, it does include variety. First Corinthians 12:4 tells us, "There are different kinds of gifts, but the same Spirit. There are different kinds of service, but the same Lord. There are different kinds of working, but the same God works all of them in all men." The writer goes on to say in verses 14-20,

> Now the body is not made up of one part but of many. If the foot should say, "Because I am not a hand, I do not belong to the body," it would not for that reason cease to be part of the body. And if the ear should say, "Because I am not an eye, I do not belong to the body," it would not for that reason cease to be part of the body. If the whole body were an eye, where would the sense of hearing be? If the whole body were an ear, where would the sense of smell be? But in fact God has arranged the parts of the body, every one of them, just as he wanted them to be. If they were all one part, where would the body be? As it is, there are many parts, but one body.

My friend Larry Randolph likes to refer to this description of the church as a galaxy of many planets revolving around the sun. We, as individuals of the great universe known as the church, must discover which orbit God has designed for us and then get in it. We should learn what our giftings are and put them to use. When we attempt to be a part of the body that we were not designed to be, we are out of our orbit and of little use to God. Unity is achieved when each part of the body functions as it was designed. Unity is the common ground we must share together in order to fulfill our calling as the church.

As individual members of Christ's church, we must accept the responsibility of our great calling. We must not be content to sit idly by, allowing others to do what we should be doing. It is imperative that each part of the body function as it was designed. Working together in unity with the rest of the body, we must proclaim the message of hope. Our hope rests in the promises of a God who sent His Son to die so that we may live forever in His glorious presence. He has sent us a "helper," the Holy Spirit, to help us fulfill the Great Commission facing each of us today and to experience the victory of walking in unity with the Almighty. We should approach the opportunity to share our hope with all the exuberance of a child opening presents at his birthday party. It is the greatest gift anyone can ever receive.

It is time to mobilize the body of Christ in unity. It is time to watch over and care for one another, to pray for and forgive one another, and reach out in love and truth to people everywhere. In His faithfulness, God has provided us with a picture of a model church in the ancient city of Thessalonica. In the coming pages, we will explore the pattern He has designed as a guide for His church to follow.

As we share the text together, I hope you will view the paintings of churches, missions, courtyards, and the West as places where we can all come together on common ground in peace, love, and hope. Witness God's love at work in the Thessalonian church and see how He is still at work in our lives today.

Together, we can make a difference.

Lord, make us an instrument of Thy peace. Where there is hatred, let us sow love; where there is despair, hope; where there is sadness, joy; where there is darkness, light. O Divine master, grant that we may not so much seek to be consoled as to console; not so much to be loved as to love. For it is in giving that we receive, it is in pardoning that we are pardoned, it is in dying that we are born again to eternal life.

—Prayer of St. Francis of Assisi

A Strong Foundation

~⁓⁓~

My wife and I joined our three-year-old grandson as he said his prayers before bedtime. As he prayed, he tossed and tumbled across the bed the entire time, even performing a somersault at one point. Little boys often have difficulty being still, even when they pray. We listened attentively as he finished blessing the entire family and were totally surprised when he closed with The Lord's Prayer. Much to our amazement, he never missed a single word or inflection throughout the entire prayer, despite the rolling and wiggling. When we asked how he learned to pray like that, he jumped up, blond hair projecting in all directions and pajamas twisted up, and replied nonchalantly, "Oh, my mommy taught me." The time our daughter had taken out of her busy schedule to teach her son how to pray had helped to build a strong foundation in his young life. Moments like these are often life's greatest rewards.

Our lives are so full of distractions. It's easy to find a million reasons why we don't have time to read a Bible story to our children or attend a church function. But the rewards for obedience are so wonderful.

When the Apostle Paul established the church in Thessalonica in about A.D. 51, he was committed to establishing it upon a strong foundation. During his second missionary journey with his companions Timothy and Silas, Paul took the time to write a letter to assure the church of his love for them. He praised them for remaining faithful despite being persecuted by the Roman government, and he reminded them of the hope of their Savior's victorious return.

Thessalonica was similar to the large cities of today's world. It was a thriving seaport located on the most important Roman highway, which extended from Rome to the Orient. A wealthy city with a population of over two hundred thousand, Thessalonica was home to many pagan religions and various cultural influences that threatened the very lives of its Christian inhabitants. Paul's letter commends the new believers for their faithfulness while under such severe persecution.

In 1 Thessalonians chapter one, we see the origins of the rock-solid Thessalonican church. Three elements come together to serve as the foundation: "Paul, Silas and Timothy, To the church of the Thessalonians in God the Father and the Lord Jesus Christ: Grace and peace to you" (verse 1).

First, we see the human element. Paul and his friends endured great hardship and much persecution because of their faith in Christ. Even when their lives were in danger, they were not deterred in their efforts to fulfill the Great Commission of spreading the gospel throughout the world. Their attitude was one of obedience. How would the people hear the gospel if they didn't proclaim it? They gladly accepted their position in the body of Christ and fulfilled their calling.

Secondly, we see the divine element. The church was established by God the Father and the Lord Jesus Christ. Verses four and five explain that God chose to establish His church with words and with the power of the Holy Spirit. Man is only able to experience the power of the gospel of Christ when God reveals Himself through His Word. Lives are dramatically changed forever when God's Word is heard and obeyed. Jesus emphasized that the power of the gospel is available to everyone: "Ask and it will be given to you; seek and you will find; knock and the door will be opened to you. For everyone who asks receives; he who seeks finds; and to him who knocks, the door will be opened" (Matthew 7:7).

The third element in the formation of the church was a blessing: "Grace and peace to you." Just as the Thessalonian believers were suffering from oppression and persecution, so many people today are starving for peace and rest in this hurried and often chaotic world we live in. The typical American family often becomes weary just trying to cope with everyday life. When both parents have jobs and shuffle children

"Come to me, all you who are weary and burdened, and I will give you rest. Take my yoke upon you and learn from me, for I am gentle and humble in heart, and you will find rest for your souls. For my yoke is easy and my burden is light" (Matthew 11:28-30).

between school, church, and extracurricular activities, stress and exhaustion become prevalent. Many young professionals are so consumed by their climb up the corporate ladder that their relationships become strained and their priorities blurred. Jesus said, "Come to me, all you who are weary and burdened, and I will give you rest. Take my yoke upon you and learn from me, for I am gentle and humble in heart, and you will find rest for your souls. For my yoke is easy and my burden is light"(Matthew 11:28-30). It is the responsibility of the church to share these valuable words and restore grace and peace to our society.

The human and divine elements coupled with the blessings of grace and peace have been so important in my own life. I was fortunate to have been raised in a Christian home where a strong foundation of faith had been passed down from generation to generation. My parents and grandparents were instrumental in sharing their faith in the importance of God's Word.

There is no greater responsibility or privilege than to build a strong spiritual foundation in our own homes with our own children and grandchildren. As Paul and his friends did not yield to the dangers surrounding them, we too must not allow the busyness surrounding our lives to interfere with our most important priorities.

As we share the gospel with those around us, we give them the opportunity to experience the most life-changing event in the history of mankind. The divine power of God in a person's life will replace fear, loneliness, and apprehension with grace, peace, and love. The Holy Spirit will bring guidance, comfort, and power in times of weakness and need. So many people are starving for peace and rest in their lives today. Like Paul, Timothy, and Silas, we must fulfill our calling. Together, we can make a difference.

There is no greater responsibility or privilege than to build a strong spiritual foundation in our own homes with our own children and grandchildren.

Three Keys to Success

Many American families had to endure extreme hardships during World War II. My uncle, Raleigh Mason, and his family were no exception. My uncle, like many young men during that day, enlisted in the Army Air Force to defend our nation after the Japanese attacked Pearl Harbor on December 7, 1941. He was only twenty years old and had spent his youth helping his dad and brothers run the family ranch. As a young man, he had heard the qualities of faith, hope, and love preached in the camp meeting revivals in west Texas, and these ideals soon became his most treasured possessions.

Prior to his deployment to Corsica, Raleigh became engaged to marry his high school sweetheart, knowing they would soon be separated by the war. In coming months he flew more than sixty combat missions in Italy, Austria, and Yugoslavia with some close calls but no serious injuries. His last flight was on April 4, 1945, when his plane took a direct hit and lost an engine. It crashed in a marshy field, and all of the surviving crewmen were taken prisoner by the Italian army, which turned them over to the Germans. Each man was stripped of his insulated clothing and all of his personal effects, then forced to march through Italy to Austria where the entire group boarded a train for a German prison camp near Munich.

Many prisoners had been in the cold and damp prison for five years. Food was extremely scarce and disease was rampant. Raleigh lost almost fifty pounds in two months and watched many around him perish. Meanwhile at home, his family had been notified of his disappearance and presumed death. It was a sad and somber time for many families in America. All they could do was support each other in prayer and hope that the war would end soon.

My uncle's faith in God gave him strength to endure the tortuous months in the prison camp. His hope for survival was fueled by his love for his family and his sweetheart, all of whom waited anxiously for his safe return. Raleigh understood the power of faith, hope, and love, and his willingness to sacrifice his own life for the lives of others defined his undaunted patriotism.

After several grueling months in the prison camp, Raleigh knew his suffering was almost over when he heard the troops of General George Patton rolling in to free the prisoners. The Allied forces had prevailed in victory. In just a few weeks he was back home, sharing the laughter of love and tears of joy with his family and friends. His faith and that of his family had truly been tested. They had endured the hard times together. The brave young soldier emerged from the perilous trials of war a mature and complete man. His hope was anchored to the promises of God, and his faith was truly rewarded. His sacrificial love for others was an example of what God wants all of us to have for one another.

We can all look to people who have exhibited the qualities of faith, hope, and love in their lives and see how the results produced endurance.

Paul wrote in 1 Thessalonians 1:3, "We continually remember before our God and Father your work produced by faith, your labor prompted by love, and your endurance inspired by hope in our Lord Jesus Christ." These three characteristics—faith, hope, and love—are the common ground shared by all effective Christians.

The Thessalonian believers were people who were certain of their faith. Hebrews 11:1 tells us, "Now faith is being sure of what we hope for and certain of what we do not see." If we have experienced the same revelation from God as they did, why should we not operate in the same realm of faith? The writer of Hebrews goes on to say in verse 6, "And without faith it is impossible to please God, because anyone who comes to him must believe that he exists and that he rewards those who earnestly seek him."

His hope was anchored to the promises of God, and his faith was truly rewarded.

We find ourselves surrounded by a world with a faith often centered upon scientific probability rather than divine revelation from God. If we are determined to make a difference in our world, we must not allow our faith in Him to be compromised.

These early Christians worked hard because they had the love of Christ in their hearts. We all know that it takes hard work to build and sustain relationships. If each of us were totally honest, most of us would have to admit that we love ourselves more than anyone or anything else most of the time. But Jesus said, "My command is this: Love each other as I have loved you. Greater love has no one than this, that he lay down his life for his friends" (John 15:12,13). Jesus gave His life that we might live eternally with Him in the presence of the Father. The majority of Christians in the early church were persecuted—sometimes even killed—for their beliefs. Even today, many missionaries and believers across the globe face religious oppression and dangerous situations as they attempt to fulfill the Great Commission.

It is the steadfastness of hope that allows us to endure. Let's face it—life is hard. We often ask ourselves if what we are doing really makes a difference. It is easy to be discouraged when we go out of our way to do something nice for someone and receive little or no thanks in return. When we are treated unfairly and things just aren't going our way, is our reaction one of hope or one of hopelessness? James 1:2-4 offers some very encouraging advice: "Consider it pure joy, my brothers, whenever you face trials of many kinds, because you know that the testing of your faith develops perseverance. Perseverance must finish its work so that you may be mature and complete, not lacking anything."

If our hope is truly in God, then we will be able to endure anything this life has to offer. God never promised us that this life would be easy. But He did promise to always be with us and to help us endure life's difficulties. He wants us to be mature and complete, for it is then that we are of the most use to Him. Together, we can make a difference.

It is the steadfastness of hope that allows us to endure.

The Power of the Good News

Watching my grandson Hunter play in his first baseball game, I could not help but observe a spiritual picture of the way God works in our lives. Hunter's team is made up of four-, five-, and six-year-old boys and girls whose exuberance for the game is both explosive and, as you might guess, at times rather clumsy—even comical.

Before the game, the players took the field to practice, running, jumping, and often tripping over their own two feet or those of their teammates. With caps tightly pulled down over their eyes and gloves in place, they began to play catch. Some would throw the ball to the wrong partner, often hitting a teammate in the head or leg, while others squatted and made designs in the sand with pebbles and blades of grass, forgetting altogether why they were there. The coaches were continually trying to get the players to focus on the game, but their attention spans didn't afford much cooperation. Soon the pregame warmup was over and the call for "Batter up!" rang through the bleachers, which were filled with proud parents and grandparents.

The players had all received the "Good News" of baseball with great power. Each had practiced knocking the ball out of the park, running the bases, and sliding fearlessly into home plate in a cloud of red dust. But as the game progressed, it was evident by their indecisiveness and sloppy fielding that they really didn't understand the object of the game and the importance of the rules. When a player finally retrieved the ball, he would hold it or struggle with his teammate over it, paying the runner absolutely no mind at all. If a plane or bird flew over the field, forget about baseball. All eyes were on the sky, no matter what was happening on the field. A player might meet a pal from school playing second base for the opposition and the two friends would stop everything and run out into right field together, pursuing a butterfly. On one hand, it was a hilariously good time. But as a granddad who used to be a pretty good ball player, I found myself frustrated about Hunter's performance—until I began to observe the coaches.

In this young age group, several coaches are allowed to be on the field with the players to help them make decisions. I noticed that each time a youngster made anything even remotely resembling a good play—whether it was falling clumsily on top of the ball or chasing it after it zoomed between their legs—he or she was patted on the back and congratulated. When the outfielder was gazing at the plane up in the sky instead of at the batter, a coach gently tapped her on the shoulder, whispering a reminder to pay attention. When a little boy cried because he didn't want to wear the intimidating wire catcher's mask, the coach hugged him and whispered something reassuring in his ear. Soon he was all smiles, taking to the dirt behind home plate. No matter how poorly he or she performed, each player was assured that everything was all right, and everyone received a high-five as a vote of confidence.

Isn't that a lot like the life of a Christian? We accept the "Good News" of the gospel and the power of the Holy Spirit in our lives. And then, just when we think we are playing by the rules and really giving it our best, we become distracted by the world around us and take our eyes off the ball. But our Helper, who is there as promised, whispers softly in our ear, convicting and correcting us, then gently guiding us back between the bases of life.

Paul wrote in 1 Thessalonians 1:4-6, "For we know, brothers loved by God, that he has chosen you, because our gospel came to you not simply with words, but also with power, with the Holy Spirit and with deep conviction. You know how we lived among you for your sake. You became imitators of us and

There is no greater common ground among believers past, present, or future than our privilege of talking personally and directly to God.

of the Lord; in spite of severe suffering, you welcomed the message with the joy given by the Holy Spirit."

The word *gospel* is translated "good news," and these Thessalonians truly believed and accepted John 3:16: "For God so loved the world that he gave his one and only Son, that whoever believes in him shall not perish but have eternal life." The good news of the death, burial, and resurrection of Christ came to them in power. Jesus promised in John 14:15-18, "If you love me, you will obey what I command. And I will ask the Father, and he will give you another Counselor to be with you forever—the Spirit of truth. The world cannot accept him, because it neither sees him nor knows him. But you know him, for he lives with you and will be in you. I will not leave you as orphans; I will come to you."

When we believe and accept the gospel, a miraculous and marvelous event takes place. The Spirit of God takes up residence in us and moves graciously upon our hearts and consciences to reveal the very heart of God. Just prior to His crucifixion, Jesus described the role of the Holy Spirit to His disciples (see John 16). He explained that when He died and returned to the Father, He would send the Holy Spirit to guide believers into all truth. Christ's death on the cross made a personal relationship with God available to everyone who believes. There is no greater common ground among believers past, present, or future than our privilege of talking personally and directly to God.

The gospel came to the Thessalonian believers with deep conviction. The Holy Spirit was sent to reveal all divine truth, convict the world of its sin, and graciously encourage a turning away from that sin. After repentance, He moves with power upon the hearts and consciences of people everywhere, bringing comfort, guidance, and assurance of acceptance into God's family.

We are members of a team guaranteed of victory. Our coach offers limitless patience and total forgiveness and the promise that, together, we can make a difference.

Imitators of the Lord

I learned so much about the value of good works when I was growing up by simply watching my dad. To this day, he is the best example of faith in motion I have ever witnessed. I recall our long summer vacation drives across Texas to visit our family. Eight hours in a car with my little brother and me asking, "Are we almost there yet?" every five minutes almost drove my parents crazy. We were so anxious to see our grandparents and play with our cousins. Anything that slowed us down only fueled more incessant questions and complaints.

But, as fate would have it, it seemed that a car was always broken down on the side of the road, and Dad would always pull over to render any assistance he could. Always a great mechanic, Dad could fix almost anything. As my brother and I sat pouting in the hot car, Dad would climb under the hood, making adjustments with greasy wrenches and fiddling with steaming hoses for the driver of a pickup truck, or hunker down in a ditch to change a flat tire for a lady who was stranded with her three children. My brother and I waited in agony, just knowing we were never going to arrive at our destination. Eventually, Dad would silently climb back in behind the wheel, covered in grease, sweat dripping down his shirt, and drive off. I never once heard him complain.

In the years to come, I accompanied Dad with a bag of groceries for a needy family someone had told him about. I watched him mow yards for widows and patch roofs and windows for neighbors after a hurricane. I saw him just sit and talk to the lonely and heartbroken elderly in the nursing home, trying to bring some joy into their day. I remember his late-night visits to the hospital, offering comfort to the sick and to their families. I heard his kind

Just as seasoning is necessary to bring out the best flavor in the foods we cook, we as Christians need to bring out the best in the people with whom we are in contact.

words of encouragement for the boys he coached on my Little League team and witnessed the time he took to teach and build confidence in each young player. I watched him share the joy of his grandson's birth and dry a mother's tears as she wept over her son's flag-draped casket, which was just back from Vietnam.

My friends, that is salt and light. That is a life modeled after our Lord. That is the role of all who are called Christians.

Paul encouraged the church in 1 Thessalonians 1:6,7, "You became imitators of us and of the Lord; in spite of severe suffering, you welcomed the message with the joy given by the Holy Spirit. And so you became a model to all the believers in Macedonia and Achaia."

Despite persecution, often even unto death, the believers in the early church were committed to being living examples of the gospel that they had joyfully accepted. It is difficult for most of us to imagine how hard it was to model Christianity in a place where the government and people were so violently opposed to it. In America, we are so fortunate to have never known that type of oppression. But when we take a broad, sweeping look at our society today, we see a spirit of hopelessness and cynicism that is very unhealthy. Apathy prevails where there is a lack of joy and hope. The church must once again ignite the hope of victory for all people.

Jesus painted a picture of how we individually as believers and collectively as the church should make a difference in our communities. In Matthew 5:13-16, He said, "You are the salt of the earth. But if the salt loses its saltiness, how can it be made salty again? It is no longer good for anything, except to be thrown out and trampled by men. You are the light of the world. A city on a

hill cannot be hidden. Neither do people light a lamp and put it under a bowl. Instead they put it on its stand, and it gives light to everyone in the house. In the same way, let your light shine before men, that they may see your good deeds and praise your Father in heaven."

When a seasoning becomes flavorless, it is of no value to the cook. Likewise, when Christians are satisfied just to occupy a pew week after week and make no effort to positively affect the world around them by sharing the joy of the gospel, they become flavorless and consequently of little or no value to God. Just as seasoning is necessary to bring out the best flavor in the foods we cook, we as Christians need to bring out the best in the people with whom we are in contact.

If you have ever driven a car at night across a vast, flat landscape in total darkness, it is easy to understand Jesus' analogy of a city on a hill. I have driven for several hours at a time across west Texas, seeing no light at all, when suddenly the glow of a town on the horizon appears. It may be fifty or more miles away, but the radiance from the lights shining together is clearly visible. It is impossible not to see it. Jesus said that our lights as Christians should glow just as brightly, glorifying our Heavenly Father for all the world to see.

There are many ways we allow our lamps to be put under a bowl. Sometimes we have an occasion to share our hope with others but choose to remain silent for fear of offending them by our faith. Sometimes we conclude that it is easier to go along with the majority and not make any waves than it is to take a stand for what we know is right. Sometimes we don't stop to help others in need because it will interfere with our own busy schedule. Sometimes

God wants our lights to shine brightly so that others will see our good works.

we simply don't want to get involved. But God wants our lights to shine brightly so that others will see our good works.

The Thessalonians remain good models for us to follow because of how they imitated Christ and were salt and light to their region of the world. Our lights grow dim and our faith weakens when we stop modeling the life of Christ. James explains how simply this principle is applied:

> What good is it, my brothers, if a man claims to have faith but has no deeds? Can such faith save him? Suppose a brother or sister is without clothes and daily food. If one of you says to him, "Go, I wish you well; keep warm and well fed," but does nothing about his physical needs, what good is it? In the same way, faith by itself, if it is not accompanied by action, is dead. But someone will say, "You have faith; I have deeds." Show me your faith without deeds, and I will show you my faith by what I do. You believe that there is one God. Good! Even the demons believe that—and shudder (James 2:14-19).

The common ground of responsibility for all Christians is to prove our faith by our actions. Helping others accomplishes two great things. First of all, it shares hope with those in need, thus glorifying God. Secondly, it strengthens our faith and fulfills our desire to please God. It makes us feel good to know that our light is shining. Together, we can make a difference.

The Pursuit of Excellence

More than 35 years ago, my grandmother gave me a short poem that she had cut out of the newspaper and placed in a small gold frame. It is now yellow and faded, but I still enjoy taking it off the shelf and reading it. I don't know who wrote the lines, but the author certainly understood the importance of Paul's words about respect.

Your Name

It came from your father, it was all he had to give

So it's yours to use and cherish as long as you may live.

If you lose the watch he gave you, it can always be replaced.

But a black mark on your name, son, can never be erased.

It was clean the day you took it and a worthy name to bear

When I got it from my father, there was no dishonor there.

So make sure you guard it wisely—after all is said and done.

You'll be glad the name is spotless when you give it to your son.

—Author Unknown

As we allow God to work in us, we share the common ground of fulfilling His purpose.

While the poem has special significance for me in this physical world, I see a spiritual significance for all Christians as well. Our very name, "Christian," came as a free gift from our Heavenly Father. When He sent His only Son to die a lonely and humiliating death on the cross, He gave all He had to give. It is the name above all other names, and it should be used with all the gratitude and reverence we can express. It must be cherished and honored as long as we live.

In 1 Thessalonians 4:1, Paul advised, "Finally, brothers, we instructed you how to live in order to please God, as in fact you are living. Now we ask you and urge you in the Lord Jesus to do this more and more." If we could pray only one prayer a day, we would do well to say, "Lord, help me to be more pleasing to you today than ever before." Our very reason for life itself is contained in this simple prayer.

God's desire is for us to continually strive to do better in our pursuit of excellence and holiness. The closer we walk with Him, the more He can use us to further His Kingdom. Part of our sanctification process requires effort on our part to be more like Jesus. Philippians 2:12-15 urges us to "…continue to work out your salvation with fear and trembling, for it is God who works in you to will and to act according to his good purpose. Do everything without complaining or arguing, so that you may become blameless and pure, children of God without fault in a crooked and depraved generation, in which you shine like stars in the universe…."

As we allow God to work in us, we share the common ground of fulfilling His purpose. Our pursuit of excellence will make us shine like stars. God seems to like things that shine, doesn't He?

In 1 Thessalonians 4:9,10, Paul commends the Thessalonian believers for their love but once again encourages them to do it "more and more." Love makes our actions and gifts useful to God. Without love, the things we do don't have much impact.

If we are able to help others who are truly in need of assistance, we can demonstrate God's love to them.

If I speak in tongues of men and of angels, but have not love, I am only a resounding gong or a clanging cymbal. If I have the gift of prophecy and can fathom all mysteries and all knowledge, and if I have a faith that can move mountains, but have not love, I am nothing. If I give all I possess to the poor and surrender my body to the flames, but have not love, I gain nothing. Love is patient, love is kind. It does not envy, it does not boast, it is not proud. It is not rude, it is not self-seeking, it is not easily angered, it keeps no record of wrongs. Love does not delight in evil but rejoices with the truth. It always protects, always trusts, always hopes, always perseveres. Love never fails (1 Corinthians 13:1-8).

Finally, in 1 Thessalonians 4:11,12, Paul writes, "Make it your ambition to lead a quiet life, to mind your own business and to work with your hands, just as we told you, so that your daily life may win the respect of outsiders and so that you will not be dependent on anybody." I think Paul closes this section of his letter this way to emphasize the importance of being a hard-working, well-respected member of society. If we win the respect of people, they are more likely to listen to us. If we are able to help others who are truly in need of assistance, we can demonstrate God's love to them.

Our loving God gives us many gifts in life and, because we are merely human, we sometimes don't recognize where they are coming from. We may lose them or squander them away, but because He is always faithful and loving, He entrusts us with yet another gift. When we are weak and stumble and cause a black mark to be placed upon our name, He is faithful to erase it if only we ask.

Oh, yes, our name was clean when we got it. It was whiter than snow— a name that only God said we were worthy to bear. Our inheritance was the free gift of a spotless name, washed in the blood of His only Son. That is the reason we pursue excellence. That is our common ground. Together, we can make a difference.

Power to Endure

My grandmother was a pioneer woman in west Texas who bravely endured life's many hardships and heartbreaks. Through faith and hope in God, she lived her eighty-four years determined to let her light shine despite the disappointments of this life. She never let her eyes stray from the reward that was to come. She dressed every day in the armor provided by God.

During her lifetime, my grandmother raised five children—three boys and two girls. Her first son died at the young age of eleven from the polio epidemic that spread uncontrollably across America. A few years later, the Great Depression hit the people of west Texas hard, and families struggled just to survive. Money and food were scarce, but my grandmother's family pulled together with neighbors and friends, sharing vegetables from their gardens and prayers of encouragement. Grandmother sewed many of her family's clothes from discarded cotton flour sacks. During these trying years, her youngest son, Bill, was diagnosed with a severe learning disability. The schools were not equipped to care for him, so he remained at home and was nurtured by his mother full-time, as he would be throughout his entire life. Their family of six shared a small, one-room frame house that was held together by little more than the lumber of love and nails of hope. My grandmother endured life's hardships by trusting in the promises of God, determined and ever hopeful.

The post-Depression years saw cotton become "king" in Texas, bringing new opportunities to many struggling families. My grandfather seized the chance to start a business storing, testing, and shipping the crops raised by the farmers in their area. Grandmother, Bill, and the eldest son, Jack, all pitched in, and the business soon prospered. It wasn't long before they added a much-needed kitchen, a bathroom, and two bedrooms to their humble frame home. But just when life was finally going their way, the country entered World War II and Jack

"Jackie boy, this life is awful hard, but some day we will all be together in Heaven and it will be worth it all."

found himself in the perilous invasion of Normandy while his two new brothers-in-law entered the service as pilots. Grandmother always attributed their safe return to four years of answered prayers.

Soon after the war, Jack returned home to work with his dad, expanding the family business. Jack married and the family was happier and more optimistic than ever, enjoying the post-war prosperity in America. The good times would soon end, however, in another devastating tragedy for my grandmother. Jack and his young bride were involved in a terrible car accident. Jack did not survive, and his expectant wife narrowly escaped with her life and that of her unborn child. I was born six months later, bringing the hope of a new life into the midst of yet another tragedy.

Within a few years, my grandfather died unexpectedly, leaving my grandmother alone for the first time in over fifty-five years to care for her constant companion and youngest son, Bill. Despite all of life's disappointments and heartaches, Grandmother remained full of hope and optimistic about the future. She was a true inspiration, and I always considered her my best friend. I learned a great deal about faith, hope, and love from the many experiences we shared. We visited each other often, and with Bill at our side, we fished many stock tanks and creeks in west Texas for catfish. We searched for Indian artifacts along the banks of the river and explored old abandoned barns and farmhouses, just enjoying being together in the beauty of God's creation.

During our outings, Grandmother loved to share family stories, remembering all of the good times. Her face would glow as she recalled some fifty-odd years in the past when her first son was so brilliant in math—the smartest boy in the one-room schoolhouse—before polio took his young life. She smiled ear to ear when she described how excited Jack was to receive her homemade cookies and bottles of Coca-Cola while dodging the bombs and bullets of the Germans. It made her proud that he always shared them with his buddies in the battalion.

She reminisced of my grandfather's many talents, how he carved out a life of his own from the age of 13, living off the land and learning many occupations and trades. "He could do anything," she would say with pride.

In all the time we spent together, I was most impressed with her optimism. I never heard a single complaint about her life. She lived every day thankful for all the blessings God had provided, focused on the victory that would someday be hers.

One cold winter night, Grandmother, Bill, and I sat together huddled around the warmth of a crackling fire in her red brick fireplace. I asked her how she had endured all the tragedies and heartaches. I was a young man in my twenties, searching for the secret of success in life and anxious to draw upon her wisdom. She slowly opened the pages of her tattered Bible to the book of 1 Thessalonians, chapter 4, and shared the story of Christ's return. The words Paul had written so long ago had obviously been a source of great comfort to her for many years. Every word was underlined and faded notes were written up and down the pages from years of meditation and study.

Her index finger, gracefully curved from years of arthritis, moved slowly beneath the words on the yellowed page as she read each line with confidence and determination. This passage had sustained her through many trials and tribulations. It was her source of strength and her power to endure. She turned to me, smiled, and said, "Jackie boy, this life is awful hard, but some day we will all be together in Heaven and it will be worth it all." I realized at that point that my grandmother had walked through this life victorious because she always remained focused on God's promise of her reward to come. She longed for the day she would be reunited with her loved ones, together forever in the presence of the Lord.

The light of hope that permeated my grandmother's life is the common ground of victory shared by all who are called according to His purpose.

Just prior to my grandmother's death, something very special occurred. I sat throughout the night next to her hospital bed as she slumbered peacefully. When she awoke the next morning, she shared with me a dream she had about Heaven. Her face glowed with joy as she began to describe the incredible light that surrounded her loved ones as she approached them through the clouds. Her husband and two sons, father and mother, and brothers and sisters who had gone on before her were all there to welcome her with open arms and smiling faces. She had heard the call of the archangel and God, in His graciousness, had given her a glimpse of her imminent reward. In a few short hours, her dream became a reality.

The light of hope that permeated my grandmother's life is the common ground of victory shared by all who are called according to His purpose. It is the hope that must be proclaimed with voices of unity.

Paul closes 1 Thessalonians 4 with a description of Christ's victorious return to earth to claim His Bride, the church. These were words of encouragement to the church there and to every believer throughout the ages. Paul explained how the same love that unites believers in this life will unite believers at the second coming of the Lord.

> For the Lord himself will come down from heaven, with a loud command, with the voice of the archangel and with the trumpet call of God, and the dead in Christ will rise first. After that, we who are still alive and are left will be caught up together with them in the clouds to meet the Lord in the air. And so we will be with the Lord forever. Therefore encourage each other with these words (1 Thessalonians 4:16-18).

All Christians, either living or dead when Christ returns, will rise to live with Him forever. When our loved ones die, we should not despair. When world events threaten us with tragedy and hopelessness, we must remember God's promises. He will transform death into everlasting life; he will turn tragedy into triumph, sickness into perfection, and hopelessness into eternal security. He never promised us that the life we have chosen would be easy, but He gave us these powerful words of comfort and reassurance so that we might share our hope with a hopeless world. It is the common ground of every believer.

Paul opens chapter five with a call for Christians to be ready for the unexpected and sudden return of Christ. So often we live as though there is no anticipation of the Lord's imminent return. Yet no one knows when Christ will return. "…for you know very well that the day of the Lord will come like a thief in the night. While people are saying, 'Peace and safety,' destruction will come on them suddenly, as labor pains on a pregnant woman, and they will not escape. But you, brothers, are not in darkness so that this day should surprise you like a thief. You are all sons of the light and sons of the day. We do not belong to the night or to the darkness. So then, let us not be like others, who are asleep, but let us be alert and self-controlled" (1 Thessalonians 5:2-6). Wouldn't it be great if we all lived each day fully prepared for His return? We can!

Paul reminds us in verse eight of the spiritual armor we have been issued to help us be prepared and endure the hardships of this life: "But since we belong to the day, let us be self-controlled, putting on faith and love as a breastplate, and the hope of salvation as a helmet." Paul's reference to our armor is more thoroughly explained in his letter to the Ephesians in chapter six. As we prepare for Christ's return, we must depend on God's strength. He has given us the power of the Holy Spirit living in us and every piece of armor we need to stand firm. It is our choice, however, whether we choose to dress in the armor each day and experience victory or to settle for something less.

God wants us ready, and He promised in Matthew 16:18 that the gates of Hades would not overcome His church. When Christ returns, the church is guaranteed victory. God wants us to wear His armor until that day and share the common ground of victory, filled with courage and hope. As we endure this life on earth in the victory of the Lord, the light of our hope will shine for all to see. Together, we can make a difference.

Encouraging Words

A few years ago, I joined some men in a prison ministry to share the gospel at one of our state's maximum security facilities. If anyone ever needed encouragement, it was these prisoners. They seldom—if ever—had any visitors, and most were very dejected and hopeless. I was somewhat apprehensive when we began to talk with the prisoners, so at first I accompanied a friend who had been there before to get accustomed to the procedure. Prison can be a very intimidating place even for a visitor.

Later that afternoon I set out on my own, visiting with the men in solitary confinement. A guard opened the door to the long, narrow corridor, and I entered the block of eight cells. As the steel door slammed shut behind me, I suddenly realized I was alone with eight men who had been convicted of murder. I was consoled by the bars that separated the cells from the hallway. I had to make the most of the short time I had been allotted, so I immediately began to walk from cell to cell, speaking to each man. No one responded until I reached the man in the seventh cell.

He was a large, imposing figure, standing about six foot four. He walked over to me and grabbed hold of the bars and inquired, "What do you want?" in a low monotone voice. I glanced toward the door at the end of the narrow hallway, hoping to be reassured of my safety by the presence of the guard. Realizing I could not see him behind the locked door, I turned back to the prisoner and told him I was just there to talk and be his friend.

"I ain't got no friends," he said as he hung his head on his chest. After a moment, I replied simply, "I am your friend, and God is your friend. He loves you."

A word of encouragement at just the right time can change impending defeat into certain victory.

"Nobody ever comes in here to just talk," he said as he walked over to a small table beside his bed. He picked up a crumpled, yellowed newspaper article and handed it to me through the bars. As I began to read, I learned that this man had been convicted in the deaths of his mother and his girlfriend. If he was trying to shock me, it was working. This was not exactly what I was prepared for. "I ain't got no friends," he said as he hung his head on his chest. I was at a loss for words. What do you say to encourage someone who has committed such a horrible crime? After a moment, I replied simply, "I am your friend, and God is your friend. He loves you."

As the prisoner slowly glanced up at me, tears began to stream down his face. We talked for almost half an hour as I presented the gospel to him and answered his questions about forgiveness. Just before I had to leave, we prayed together as he repented of the terrible things he had done and invited Jesus into his heart. I never saw or heard from him again. I was given one chance to encourage him. All I know is that he had a new hope in his heart and a smile on his face as I was summoned away down the long, narrow corridor. I will never forget the echoing sound as the steel door slammed shut and locked behind me as I left.

Paul closes his first letter to the Thessalonians by writing, "Therefore encourage one another and build each other up, just as in fact you are doing" (1 Thessalonians 5:11). I am reminded of the marathon runner who collapses in total exhaustion prior to crossing the finish line. With the cheers and encouragement of friends on the sideline, he somehow gets up and musters enough energy to finish the race. A word of encouragement at just the right time can change impending defeat into certain victory.

Paul lists sixteen ways to share the common ground of encouragement with others in verses 11 through 24:

1. "Build each other up." Look for ways to encourage and support others. Discover qualities you appreciate in them, and support them with your words and actions.

2. "Respect those who work hard among you, who are over you in the Lord and who admonish you." Look for ways to serve in your church and to cooperate with your leaders.

3. "Hold them in the highest regard in love because of their work." Support them with your appreciation. Let them know how much their leadership, teaching, and hard work help you and your family.

4. "Live in peace with each other." We don't agree with each other all of the time, but we really should respond to others in love rather than react out of self-centeredness. We must find ways to work out our differences and come together in a united effort.

5. "Warn those who are idle." Those who are satisfied to simply fill a seat and not actively participate in the church need to be encouraged to use their talents. Invite them to help you in a project or service. Explain to them that they aren't being all God has designed them to be.

6. "Encourage the timid." Some people lack confidence due to inexperience. Or they may be idle due to shyness, even though they have a willingness to serve. Help them to understand that God's promises are for them, too, and that the body is not complete without them. Model ways in which they can begin to participate.

7. "Help the weak." Be a friend to the weak and encourage them with kind words and actions. Pray for them, give them support, and let them know that you truly care about their condition.

8. "Be patient with everyone." The fact is, some people really try our patience. In these instances, it is important that we remain calm and respond out of love rather than react from our own self-centered point of view. We are all different and we, too, require the patience of others at times.

9. "Make sure that nobody pays back wrong for wrong." Sometimes we feel like getting revenge when we have been mistreated or wronged by another. But Jesus said to do good to those who wrong you. Vengeance belongs to the Lord. Our command is to love one another unconditionally, as God loves us.

10. "Be joyful always." Even in the midst of life's troubles and heartaches, we need to know that God is in control. He has promised that all things work together for good for those who love Him.

11. "Pray continually." God resides in every believer by the power of the Holy Spirit. He is always with us to hear us and guide us—and even to help us pray. He desires open lines of communication with us at all times.

12. "Give thanks in all circumstances." If we are certain that God is in control and if we allow Him to control our steps, it is easy to give thanks. If we are trusting in ourselves, it's often impossible to be thankful. It is important to note that Paul wrote to be thankful "in" all circumstances, not "for" everything that happens to us. Bad and evil things don't come from God, but when we find ourselves in those circumstances, we can thank God that He is there with us and that He will accomplish good things in bad circumstances.

13. "Do not put out the Spirit's fire." The power of the Holy Spirit in our lives is the blessing of our individual gifts and the ability to hear from God. Paul warns us that when the Holy Spirit nudges us to do or say something, we should not ignore the instruction. This is the way God accomplishes His works through us, and it is critical that we cooperate with Him.

14. "Do not treat prophecies with contempt." We should receive God's Word from those who speak for Him, but at the same time we need to be cautious and "test" everything according to the scripture. If we think we disagree with what someone says, we should first check the Word. We can then accept what is true and reject what is false. The Word of God is the ultimate test.

15. "Avoid every kind of evil." The world tempts us in every way possible. We must focus on obeying God and avoiding situations that are certain to be a temptation. This reinforces the need to be in constant prayer. When we find ourselves in a tempting situation, we can immediately talk to God about it.

16. "May God himself, the God of peace, sanctify you through and through. May your whole spirit, soul and body be kept blameless at the coming of our Lord Jesus Christ. The one who calls you is faithful and he will do it." To experience peace and victory, we cannot simply allow God to control a portion of our life while we hold on to other areas that we want to control ourselves. Our process of sanctification requires our willingness to allow God to be involved in every aspect of our life, spirit, soul, and body. God wants all of us, not just a couple of hours on Sunday morning.

God wants His children to encourage others as He encourages us. "'For I know the plans I have for you,' declares the LORD, 'plans to prosper you and not to harm you, plans to give you hope and a future.'"

It's important that all Christians agree on the necessity of these sixteen principles outlined by Paul. Encouraging words change lives. If we put these principles into practice, our light will shine like the city on a hill, people will see our good works, and God will be glorified. God wants His children to encourage others as He encourages us. "'For I know the plans I have for you,' declares the LORD, 'plans to prosper you and not to harm you, plans to give you hope and a future. Then you will call upon me and come and pray to me, and I will listen to you. You will seek me and find me when you seek me with all your heart'" (Jeremiah 29:11-13). God wants us to share our hope and our future.

Encouraging words are so important and can do so much to change lives. While opportunities like visiting prison don't come along every day, each of us can share kind words that help to brighten the lives of others where we live and where we work. Here are a few ideas:

"You really did that well; good job!"

"That was a great sermon."

"That meant so much to my family and me."

"Thanks for teaching our kids in Sunday school; I know it takes real dedication."

"Thanks for caring."

"You certainly made my day!"

"You're such a great mom!"

"I've been praying for you."

"Thank you."

"You look great!"

"I'm sorry; please forgive me."

"You're so smart!"

"I'll always love you."

"God loves you."

Everyone needs to hear words of encouragement. Paul knew that life would be hard, and he emphasized the need to build people up. The world would be a much better place to live in if people were more encouraging and less critical.

It's time to let our lights shine. It's time to watch over and care for one another. It's time to pray for one another and to forgive one another. It's time to reach out in love and truth to people everywhere. It's time to put on the armor God has provided and walk in the strength of His power. As Christians, it's time to do everything "more and more." That is our common ground and, together, we can make a difference.